Visit the
LIBERTY
BELL

By James Francis

Gareth Stevens
Publishing

Please visit our website, www.garethstevens.com. For a free color catalog of all our high-quality books, call toll free 1-800-542-2595 or fax 1-877-542-2596.

Library of Congress Cataloging-in-Publication Data

Francis, James.
Visit the Liberty Bell / James Francis.
    p. cm. — (Landmarks of liberty)
Includes bibliographical references and index.
ISBN 978-1-4339-6394-0 (pbk.)
ISBN 978-1-4339-6395-7 (6-pack)
ISBN 978-1-4339-6392-6 (library binding)
1. Liberty Bell—History—Juvenile literature. I. Title.
F158.8.I3.F73 2012
973—dc23

                      2011025388

First Edition

Published in 2012 by
Gareth Stevens Publishing
111 East 14th Street, Suite 349
New York, NY 10003

Copyright © 2012 Gareth Stevens Publishing

Designer: Andrea Davison-Bartolotta
Editor: Therese Shea

Photo credits: Cover, p. 1, back cover (all), (pp. 2–3, 21, 22–23, 24 flag background), (pp. 4–21 corkboard background), pp. 9, 11 (inset), 17 (main) Shutterstock.com; p. 5 Ron and Patty Thomas/Photographer's Choice/Getty Images; pp. 7, 17 (inset) MPI/Getty Images; pp. 11 (main), 13, 15 SuperStock/Getty Images; p. 19 Hulton Archive/Getty Images; p. 20 William Thomas Cain/Getty Images.

Printed in the United States of America

CPSIA compliance information: Batch #CW12GS: For further information contact Gareth Stevens, New York, New York at 1-800-542-2595.

Contents

Words in the glossary appear in **bold** type the first time they are used in the text.

The Sound of Freedom

A ringing bell means many things. Some bells tell us what time it is. Others announce a special event. One famous bell doesn't ring anymore. However, its past ringing announced key events in US history. Some stories say it was rung at the first public reading of the Declaration of Independence. Today, this bell is called the Liberty Bell.

People still visit the Liberty Bell today in Philadelphia, Pennsylvania. It remains a **symbol** of freedom for the United States.

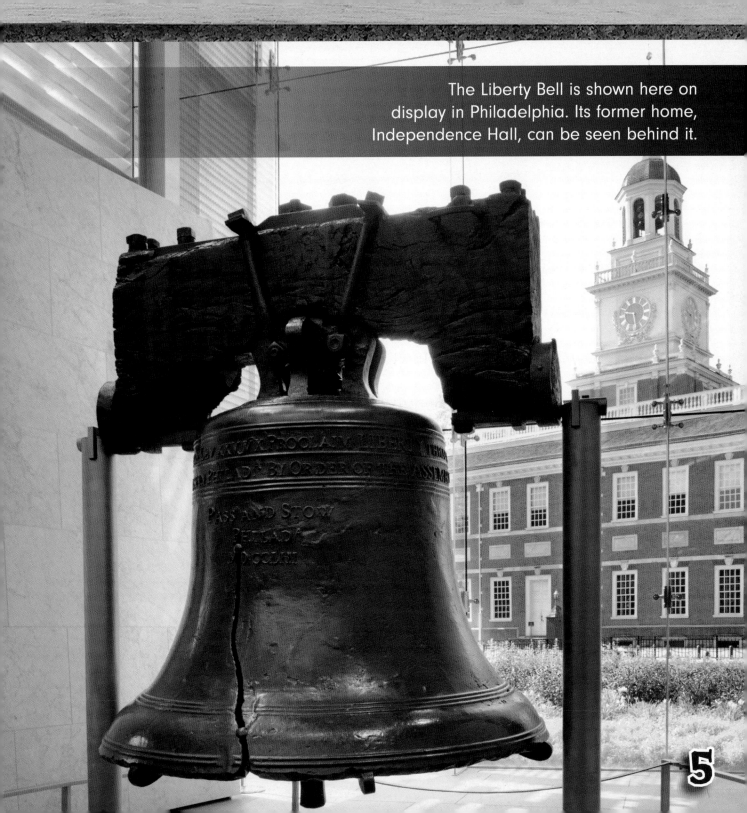

The Liberty Bell is shown here on display in Philadelphia. Its former home, Independence Hall, can be seen behind it.

Honoring William Penn

Pennsylvania was a colony founded by William Penn in 1681. Penn wanted Pennsylvania colonists to have freedom of **religion**. He wanted them to have a say in their government, too. Few colonies provided these rights at that time.

Fifty years after the colony was founded, the General **Assembly** of Pennsylvania ordered a bell to be **cast** in London, England. The bell was to hang in the Pennsylvania **State House** in Philadelphia. The bell, then called the state house bell, arrived in 1753.

Tell Me More!

Today the Pennsylvania State House is called Independence Hall.

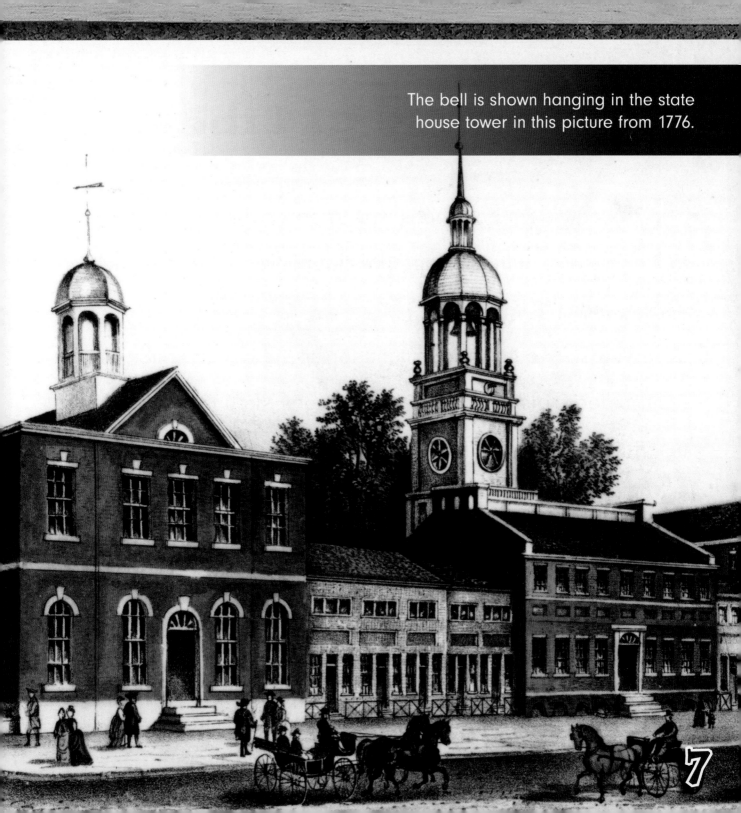

The bell is shown hanging in the state house tower in this picture from 1776.

7

The Sound of Liberty

The new state house bell was large. It was 12 feet (3.7 m) around at the bottom. The clapper, or ringer, weighed 44.5 pounds (20 kg).

Words were **inscribed** at the top of the bell to honor William Penn's ideas. They said: "**Proclaim** Liberty throughout all the land unto all the **inhabitants** thereof." These words mean that each time the bell is rung, it should remind Americans of their freedom. But the first time the bell rang, it broke!

Also inscribed on the bell are these words: "By Order of the Assembly of the **Province** of Pensylvania for the State House in Philada." Notice the spelling used at that time for Pennsylvania and the short form of Philadelphia.

The colonists paid about $225 for the state house bell. That would be about $36,500 today!

...ll ALL THE LAND UNTO ALL THE INHA...
...F THE PROVINCE OF PENSYLVANIA F...

Try, Try Again

Two craftsmen, John Stow and John Pass, recast the bell. They used metal from the first bell and added a bit more copper to make it stronger. However, some people disliked the way the second bell sounded. So the craftsmen tried again. A few people still weren't pleased by the new bell's ringing and ordered another one from London.

When the fourth bell arrived, it didn't sound any better than Stow and Pass's bell. Their bell remained in the state house. It was rung to call the assembly together and to announce news and special events.

Tell Me More!

The bell ordered from London didn't go to waste. It was placed in the state house and used to ring out the time.

If you visit the Liberty Bell, you can see the names of the craftsmen who worked on the second bell—John Stow and John Pass.

Ringing Out the Old Government

Each time the bell rang, it **signaled** changes in the colonies. At that time, they were governed by England. But many colonists became unhappy. They thought they could govern themselves better. The state house bell rang when England passed two hated taxes—the Sugar Act in 1764 and the Stamp Act in 1765.

Beginning in 1775, leaders from the American colonies began meeting in the Pennsylvania State House. They talked about ways to gain more freedom from England.

The sound of the state house bell told the colonists of important events. This is an artist's idea of the scene when the bell was rung on July 4, 1776.

Ringing In the New Country

The colonial leaders who met in Philadelphia called themselves the Second Continental Congress. They decided to break away from England. Thomas Jefferson, one of the members of Congress, wrote the Declaration of Independence to announce the new nation's freedom. Some believe that the bell in the state house was rung on July 8, 1776. It called the colonists to hear the declaration read aloud in public for the first time.

However, the bell was removed from Philadelphia in 1777. That's when the British captured the city.

Tell Me More!

The state house bell may have been rung in 1775 to tell of the first battle of the American **Revolution**, the Battle of Lexington and Concord.

People feared the British would melt the state house bell to make cannonballs. They hid it in a church in Allentown, Pennsylvania.

A New Freedom

After the American Revolution, the state house bell was rung each year on George Washington's birthday and the Fourth of July, and for elections and other events.

In the 1830s, the state house bell took on a new meaning. Many Americans were beginning to fight for an end to slavery. These **abolitionists** remembered the words about freedom for all on the bell. They used it as a symbol for their cause. They were the first to call the bell the "Liberty Bell."

Tell Me More!

A small crack in the Liberty Bell was repaired in 1846. It cracked again that year when it was rung on Washington's birthday.

Pennsylvania State House
bell tower

William Lloyd Garrison's abolitionist newspaper, *The Liberator*, was the first to use the term "Liberty Bell."

William Lloyd Garrison

17

Traveling Bell

After the **American Civil War**, slavery ended. However, anger remained on both sides. People wondered if the states could ever be truly united again. To remind people of the freedom they were lucky to have, the Liberty Bell was sent to many places for people to see.

The Liberty Bell's last trip was in 1915. Then it traveled back to its home at the state house. It's still gently rung on the Fourth of July. However, its message of freedom for all rings out clearly every day.

Tell Me More!

Another bell, called the Justice Bell, was made to look like the Liberty Bell. It was a symbol of the women's rights movement.

In 1885, the Liberty Bell traveled by train to New Orleans, Louisiana. The men shown here went with it as guards.

19

Visiting the Liberty Bell

Today, the Liberty Bell is found in the Liberty Bell Center in Philadelphia. The center is open to visitors year-round. Behind the bell is a wall of glass. Through the glass, visitors can see the Pennsylvania State House, now called Independence Hall.

These buildings and several others are part of Independence National Historical Park. The park educates people about the country's beginnings and honors the rights and freedoms that we enjoy.

The Liberty Bell Center is located on Market Street in Philadelphia, between 5th and 6th Streets.

Fun Facts about the Liberty Bell

Weight:

about 2,080 pounds
(944 kg)

Made of:

mostly copper and tin.
It also has small amounts
of lead, zinc, arsenic,
gold, and silver.

Did You Know?

The bell's crack was made
deeper on purpose so that the
two sides of the crack wouldn't
touch each other when rung.

Hangs from:

a wooden frame made from
an American elm
(it's never been replaced)

Glossary

abolitionist: one who fights to end slavery

American Civil War: the war fought in the United States from 1861 to 1865

assembly: people gathered for a common purpose, such as making laws

cast: to form something using a mold

inhabitant: one who lives in a place

inscribed: having words cut into a surface

proclaim: to announce something in public

province: an area of a country

religion: a belief in and way of honoring a god or gods

revolution: the overthrow of a government

signal: to let someone know something using a sign or action

state house: a place where lawmakers gather to make decisions

symbol: something that stands for something else

For More Information

Books

Firestone, Mary. *Celebrate America: A Guide to America's Greatest Symbols.*
Mankato, MN: Picture Window Books, 2010.

Magaziner, Henry Jonas. *Our Liberty Bell.* New York, NY: Holiday House, 2007.

Websites

Liberty Bell Center
www.nps.gov/inde/liberty-bell-center.htm
Plan your trip to visit the Liberty Bell.

Liberty Bell Museum
www.libertybellmuseum.com/resources/faqs.htm
Read the most commonly asked questions about the bell as well as their answers.

Symbols of U.S. Government: The Liberty Bell
bensguide.gpo.gov/3-5/symbols/libertybell.html
Read more facts about the Liberty Bell.

Index